The
Winged
Life

Judith A. Hartley

He who binds to himself a joy
Does the winged life destroy;
But he who kisses the joy as it flies
Lives in eternity's sunrise.

William Blake, *Miscellaneous Poems and Fragments*

In Appreciation

Though poetry is often a solitary pursuit, several friends have encouraged me over the years. Father Edward J. Farrell, Dr. John Schneider, and Julie Chai (who verged on being a nag) were my major guardian angels. Of course, I can't forget Rebecca Chown, my editor, who bubbled over, saying, "Your poetry knocks my socks off!" I thank and bless them for their belief in me and the "gift of words." Thank you especially to the Lord for his presence in my work.

Dedication

To all those I love,
all those I have touched
with my life
in any way,
I give this gift,
this gift of Self.

Table of Contents

Preface

Preface

We return to what we have always known. From childhood, babyhood, I had a certain conception, intuition, mystery concerning nature, trees, sky, water, birds – all creatures great and small. Vague, a dimmed perception that the key to my existence lay in those wildflowers haphazard by the roadway, that tree bending double in the storm, that flash of lightning over the water, the ominous thunder that both frightened and excited, the hummingbird whirring and poised over my grandmother's roses. Surely there was something there, something hinted at, something I could not pursue but which would reveal itself as I grew into womanhood.

It has. And it continues to unfold because my eyes are still those of a child.

I see in poetry the distillation of Self. In poetry I have left mother, father, sister, children, and cling to nothingness. And there, in that clear space, a few words are spoken, linger on the air. These are my words, my gift, my – Self. More than a picture, more than a scene, more than an utterance or a human sound. And so, no matter where my art takes me, no matter what medium I pick up, always will I be a poet making sounds.

As I live in a mystery, I tiptoe through space, I touch the air with light fingers. My eyes gaze but do not possess. My mind considers but does not ponder. Nothing eludes me and yet everything does. Perhaps yesterday will float in on today. Maybe tomorrow is even now present. If today is a poem, so was yesterday. I cease writing essays and live on a scattering of words. The seashells in my mind contain the ocean but I hold them at a certain distance so they whisper rather than roar. Mine is a small existence, a brief time of whispering. I was here once, I spoke a few words, and left. Without possessing a thing, I caress the universe and carry it within me. My minute life swims in an eternity of space.

I live the winged life.

Section One:

Window on the Sky

Among We Ordinary People

March is brutal
in its ordinary line
of porous snow
its subterfuge
its weak lament
among
we ordinary people.

It issues a cold challenge.
Each gray day
another call
from a weary bed
to a weary day
to a duty,
a people.

March is brutal
for ordinary people,
without violets,
given no color,
no form, no voice,
only a duty,
a people.

March is brutal.
Even these words lack
leafy detail or delicacy
only the language
of bones
without feather or flesh
their subterfuge
merely
a weak lament
among
we ordinary people.

I Invite You

I invite you:
Climb this proffered tree
branch after branch
a sturdy browned ladder
hung by the sun
rung after rung after rung
        splintered and real.

I invite you:
Climb my steady tree –
        Up – Up.
Suspended in my framework
as you work your way skyward
                        sunward.

Your hand grasping bark
        perceives earth, roots, a throbbing.
As you peer down
the ground undulates
like a mint wave,
your mind froths giddy and white.

The sky topaz blue
        golden azure – a gem
scattering sight
        gold dropped, strung out
pebbles in the sky,
        the light interiorizes
as your eye penetrates cloud.

Still you touch raw bark – coarseness.
Still you touch me,
                earthling, rooted.
Still you are of round earth

but airy to behold!
Traversing my branches
branch after branch after branch
rung after rung after rung
singed by the sun
my sturdy brown ladder
           carries your song
              and returns it
                 to the earth
                    throbbing.

A Link on Stoney Creek

An encounter
by a stone wall
smooth and unexpected.

Two horses on a brown curve
a shoulder of stone
a greater living, somehow,
      than oak, creek, sky
their eye a dimmed consciousness
a reminder remotely man
meets
      greets
my human mind and hand,
a link between
      wall, tree, sky
thick winter coat, hoof
      innocent eye
nuzzles down for sugar,
                carrot
finds only human flesh
on his breathy mouth.

Trails saliva,
      hair
and sees silently:
Field, wall, sky
human flesh
mine
      his.

Look It in the Eye

November day.
How strangely sullen it is –
scowling, furrowed brow
spitting in my face.

Can I pretend nonchalance,
sun or shadow – who cares?
While inwardly
      I crouch low
in this dim corner of room
pleading for light,
even snow, a clearer image
on which to hang a day.

Now I have learned –
November takes courage
      (not as May or June).
Its sullen countenance
insults and derides
but I have made a truce with it,
a begrudging sort of friend.

Let me remember other Novembers
and stare it down.
Perhaps it is a paper lion
I can taunt and play with.
Perhaps not. I'll try.
Look it in the eye.

Transition Months

Transition months,
May and October –
I am strung out between them
like a marred pink wooden bead
skuttling back and forth
on a kindergartener's string.

Transition months,
my fleshy bead strung tight
dropping with sinking barometer
undone by shuddering leaf
and fallen bird
waiting – .

Transition months
imposing a strained note
on my strung-out rhythm
I wait –
for summer's lapping light,
the silence of snow.
Rest.

Cider Sun

Sip the sun
slowly slipping through laced leaves
     finely strung veins
          permeating into cool consciousness.

Hold it here in my mouth
taste the cider green globules
     trickling into my lungs
to the warm mauve breast, the curved fingertips,
     the round white abdomen,
          through the thighs and further still
not culminating at my feet
     but reaching further into the earth
     rooting me here
a libation of the gods
     a green gold stream
          a river to the sky.

Yarn Bud

Every room
receives the sunlight
a little differently.

And I sit, receive,
and watch
dappled light patterns
like a pussycat
with wide golden eyes.

Spring is unraveling
      its chartreuse yarn bud
           before me
               rolling it out
and my eyes trip and tease
         the light
              playing with it
delighting in
the playful frivolity
of a pussycat
with wide golden eyes
and this
        her first spring.

Crazed Splendor

The crazed splendor
                    of nature's spillings
its wildness throbbing
in the agony throes of creation.

The round grape bursting
the blossom spewing forth
the clouds banked thick and heavy
the piercing blue expanse
the trees stretching aching limbs.

All this piercing beauty
ripping, tearing open my breasts,
exposing the heart
                    beating
                                        ceaselessly beating
throbbing crimson red and straining with life,
longing for death, the quiet grave,
ceaseless, ceaseless,
                    pound, pound
across the huge expanse of blue ether.

I am alive. I AM PAIN.

To my dear Tracy,

We Have the Doves This Summer

We have the doves this summer
though it is cold and dry,
they add a warm touch
gentle, grey and shy.

We have the doves this summer
warming the worn wood,
they lie plumped on the porch
as we knew they would.

Deep, deep inside me
they have found a private place,
I am partaking today
of their gentleness and grace.

I watch the doves of summer
a woman soft as down
reclining on her pillows
as the sun goes round.

We have the doves this summer
though it is cold and dry,
they add a warm touch
gentle, grey and shy.

The Beach

Eyes flicker
pulses tick
the pink sand glows
the slender reeds bend
another day
breathes another sigh
as the beach stretches
rosy limbs
and the day
seeps into it.

Cedar Waxwings

Waxwings – cedar grayed, crested
the maroon berries suck you
from the sky
         thirty large
to swoop, group, bodies laid backward
skinny boned feet seeking twig.

With shading subtly defying the definite
you crowd, blend as one
           all thirty of you
one swoop of feather and feet
reaching the branch anticipate.

And I
      crouch forward, muscles creamed,
       belly buttoned and rolled jelly tight
follow your mindless besiegement
on berries glossy and sure
skimmed and held, bounced upward
                beakward
gulped in round unison.

You are a crowd of one
     and as you loosen
          flutter
the sky flattens to retrieve you
feasted, berried,
       bellyward to the sun.

The Severe Element

Silent the snow,
silent and weighty.

Encompass, enclose, inhabit
this brief space.

Formed limbs
now mantled, malleable.

I grasp you, Snow
(the severe element)
better than rain or spring.

You oppress and regress
the intellect drawn into
your white space
       of disbelief.

I cease believing
in blood, flesh –
I believe only in you,
       Snow.

Severe silent element,
the comfort you give
lies unsought, unimagined.

Yet I grasp your cold weight
as my substance,
white with disbelief,

     Believes.

As a Tree

These inscrutable trees
insisting on something
no longer green, no longer round
something angular but smooth
something to be breathed, a realness
a realness the rain, the mist, the wetness
intensifies and deepens
as the earth blackens and softens and exudes.

These inscrutable trees
enduring the rain, the mist, the wetness
say more in their silence
than a thousand cornfields in sun
especially at night
when they loom larger
darker,
breathing cold
and hollow.

I listen to their breathing,
my own breath soft – still – white,
my gray flesh rain-wetted, obscured
listens to their breathing
darker, colder now
in the night
in the rain.

If I could breathe this tree
then I too could last
could endure
could transform myself
could be all things
without moving
simply by breathing

darker – clearer – colder
as a tree
inscrutable
insisting on something
breathing a realness
intensified and deepened
black and soft and large
inscrutable
as a tree.

Ducks

Everything is stillness
my head turns, remains there
breath stilled.

My mind a smooth gray glide
thoughts like small ducks
on icy film.

Smooth. Clean. Cold.
The long sun streams
into unflicked eyes.

Shock – still the moment
frozen onto my skin –
a sliver, a dry crackle:

A memory hard with ease.

This Small Fallen Circle

Pre-dawn darkness
a vague autumn presence
dark gold – heavy.
I lie crumpled and barely conscious
to softened air, flowing blood,
hair spread in a flower of warmth.

This semi-state enters
into floating colors
that flurrying, scurrying, scud
like fragments, curling
gold and rust scraps
tossed up in a warm October rain.

Pre-dawn darkness
I strain into it, one knee
pressed into the sheets,
one mind floating free behind filmy eyelids,
the hair sensuous and gold
above a langorous curving form.

This suspended life –
here I am – open
to the lidded mind but
closed to the striving form
here in pre-dawn autumn.
The womb's webby water
laps at my limbs
while my mind is being formed
by gold fragments
filtering in on my mother's last mood.

Loomy force in the wind,
the fertile earth

I dropped into decomposes
beneath my tucked form.
Fawn fragile
in my small fallen circle
the arc I traversed yesterday is
a dim meaning in my form
yet this mind holds womb water,
hangs suspended

in the pre-dawn darkness
of another age.

There Is a Certitude Here

There is a certitude here
a dark breathing
a grave play.

There is a quiet here
broad and deep
a soft steady beating
sameness diverse
one true lovely meandering
on green sprung ground.

A certitude wide
                as meadow expanse
an exacting landscape
(no drifting clouds)
expansive but definite
without the obscurity
a large gaze can envision.

There is a deep well here
a hidden spring
                waters the meadow
a promise of limitless years of green,
a dark breathing
imbues the ordinary meadow
with poignantly ordinary life.

There is a certitude here
a dark breathing
a grave play.

If You Ask Why

I dwell here in pain and peace,
a window on the sky
a door into the earth.

If you ask why,
I will answer:
The sky is a vast expanse,
a blue radiant realm.
It is mine.

If you ask why,
I will answer:
The earth is a wound
I lie in
sheltered.
It is mine.

I dwell here in pain and peace,
a window on the sky
a door into the earth.

If you again ask why,
I will remain silent.

Section Two:

Walk the Dark Path

This Lengthy Breathing Road

This lengthy breathing road
rising up out of –
        climbing eastward
from the green cleaving valley.

Mountain road, a brown breath
my sun-eyed level
        narrowing, banked in silver
molten light, a thin stream
        feeble
trembles on my form.

A lengthy breathing road
my mountain, rising eastward
        the sunny residual
        flickers, snipes, flares
like a sputtering candle
on this hard road
        (years of it)
stretching eastward into a dimming storm
when it reaches me
        the wind a lengthy breathing
hard on my broad path
I will flicker
                drop
                        and go out.

Sunday Afternoons

Sunday afternoons are often
a muttering curse
and the God
of oranges, coffee,
and Holy Sacrifice is lost
in the Sunday movie.

Educational TV lacks my attention
but keeps muttering
just the same.

Hold me.

My Priests

My priests
offer Holy Sacrifices
every dawn
and hold Christ
in their hands.

I am only a girl
and sometimes forget
Christ is
in the bread
and look only
at their hands.

My confessions are strangely silent
and my poems are the only forgiveness.

To Scott,

This Boy and I

Those early years were a stumbling forth
into half-truths and confusion.

No debutante I, poised on a marble staircase.
More likely, pushed down the worn passageway
of my mother's mistakes
into an early commitment.

I chose with half-sealed eyes
before I knew there was a choice,
this brief marriage, this young son, this boy.

The years shuttled painfully by –
I walked on with this boy. Alone.
Two of us, but Alone.

Truth – Wholeness – Allness
tempted me, caught at me, intrigued me.
I struggled – searched – pursued –
took many wrong turns.

Faltering many times over
until the relatives, even,
seemed to watch with embarrassed
and averted eyes.

Now this boy flies his version
of Truth across the skies
as my pen scratches
a paper chase into the heavens.

I have made my way here
to this town, this house, this decade.

Truth brought me here –
to this place –
not desert but rolling hills
greenly serenely lush – hills of wholeness.

We live simply – mother, son,
both young creatures in this young galaxy.
We work out our own small parcel of wholeness
in this universe
of multiplicity.

We ask fewer questions now
for the All seems more obvious and needs
only to be addressed with the eyes.

We own the steady vision, firm hand, clear voice.
We realize our Aloneness, this boy and I –
we know it now as we knew it then –
many years ago.

To Scott,

Manhood & Mahogany

Son, your veneer is thick, dark, polished
manhood and mahogany.

You never asked much of me,
my motherhood a fragile thing
I struggled to grow into,
my young spring sapling
swinging a gentle protective arc
over your sturdy offshoot.

I was competent; I was efficient.

Your clothes were scrubbed clean,
your young limbs were washed.
You were my first boy doll
coming three years after I set aside Melissa,
a blond beauty,
for you, a dark living.

My fingertips transmitted
efficiency.
At seventeen I knew my house
was not in order
but, by God,
you would be.

Now you are.
At twenty your hands already smoothly worn, competent,
your mind made up,
you handle life well,
efficiency engrained,
mother and son.

You never asked much of me.
My motherhood was
a fragile thing.

To my children,

Imprinted

My tragedies are private,
carried in a low-slung
                    uterine cradle
and expelled with a gasp,
one long drawn-out sigh.

My two female forms,
in my mind still
                  fighting for breath,
grasping and sucking,
clenched fists upraised,
                      issuing a challenge.

My first manchild tunneled through
                        into legitimate territory
but these two lusty waifs
leave my warm dough ring
                  for straight sterile arms,
their umbilical cords singed and branded.

My womb carries the imprint of their form,
it remains like a sworled fingerprint,
                      a smudged reminder
of flesh touched
              and left behind.

Party

I had a party last night.
Not everybody came though it was
       good enough.
The elephants cluttered up the living room.
We arranged our martinis in gay array around them
and fed them olives which they didn't seem to enjoy.
Maybe it was the pimentos.

Now I am cleaning up.
This super-size baggy lacks the proper strength.
The elephants keep bumping against my chest
       as I carry them.

I never was much of a swinger.

A Dreariness Here

There is a dreariness here
a damp wet look
between the eyes.

I drive over washboard roads
see three scattered housewives
all in a quarter of an hour
all hippy and morose
limping to the mailbox
in droopy slacks and floppy blouses.

This could be 1929 as well as 1979
a timeless dreariness
the housewives washday limp
a dribbling comatose walk to the mailbox.

Depressions mark no time.
They obliterate postmarks
even as the mail arrives.

Dark Companion

Finally snowing –
each snowflake tinged
with grief.
Darkness coming and going
      a passing cloud
      making its presence known.
I dare not sleep
      for waking brings
      such heaviness
almost obscuring me
with its pain.
Tomorrow is seldom better
so hope is dimmed.
Yesterday was harsh
      today more subdued
      still – an anguish.

Resting here
breathing in and out
    palpable grief
    dark companion
    on a long journey
    a night of vigilance
a scattering of syllables
      few words –
          a heartache.

Lacking Reckless Abandon

It's Sunday all day long,
lengthy lonesome Sunday –
(this poor lil' motherless child).

I do battle against memories
      of past skirmishes
        well-fought, mostly won.

I am scarred – I am scared.
Strongest in all the broken places,
warding off all the gobbledegooks
with quick moves.

Lengthy lonesome Sunday –
I have the leisure to mourn
so I do
but sadly lacking the reckless abandon
of youth to pain
      or pleasure.

Maybe I'll end up one of these days
like the old ladies who smile at apples
in the produce section
instead of the tragic dame
I once fancied myself.

(this poor lil' motherless child.)

Sustaining Wounds

We seem to be wandering
through inconsistencies
which are becoming
so recurrent
that we can almost predict
our unpredictableness
with dark certainty
by the deep wounds
we are sustaining
within us.

If You Were Always with Me

If you were always with me
my vital fountain
would spew out
                    poetry
by the mouthful.

And though you are
            not always with me
the long silences
                    between us
pungent and darkly rich
grow strange wildflowers
in my mind.

So I do not quibble
                    between a sometimes
                                    and always.

Whatever we have
fills the day
with poetry and color
sharpening the landscape
into singular images
dropping away into a deep night
we orbit the earth
and gaze with outstretched limbs
heaven's periphery.

To Alixann and Angela,

I Gave Them Life

At least I gave them life,
those two little waifs
who forced themselves
into my December calendar
eight years apart
and still counting.

I never knew
I could keep them
  thinking they must
  be given away
to satisfy the authorities
who took care
of such things.

At least I gave them life.
I held them first
and loved their tiny perfection,

Knowing I could not be
the mother each needed,
I gave them away.

Afterwards is a long time –
my heart shattered
into a thousand different pieces.

As I gave away my lifeblood,
something in me died.
I never said good-bye –

To Debra,

Leafy Green My Bower

Green leafy green my bower
impinging on my inner space
let it – Come!
Green space, come fill fill
       fill.

The deck stretches outside this room
peeling, sorely in need of paint,
a basket of flourishing petunias
draws my eye up.

I need this sheltered room
      cooled but green, a bower,
persistent trees crowding the deck,
purple petunias, crimson purple life.

This summer lingers far too long.
I shout at it to "Go – go!"
So much heat, intense, prolonged,
sudden violent storms…

A small sailboat carelessly tossed –
a friend's body washed up on the beach,
I have had enough of it.

Summer has passed for me.
I am here in my cool greeny bower
      though sunscreens still line
      the drugstore shelves
      and children's voices drift up
      from the beach.

Green cool green living leaf
you are my last remnant
from a summer sour with grief.
Come, enter my room –
persistent green, I wait for you.

Come Catch My Tears

Still tears –
after all these years
still tears.

No longer will I weep them
          solitary.
Too many years of that.

Now is the time for healing,
the closing over of festering
          wounds.

I need someone to catch my tears
fallen so heedlessly on barren ground
for so many years.

Is there someone there?

See – I have been hiding so long.
Come find me – I need to be found.
I have been leaving so many clues
          but no one is looking
          for clues
          or for me.

They think long ago
I set myself free.

No, I am not a Houdini,
but I have left clues –
like Hansel and Gretel
I sprinkle my breadcrumbs.

I forget how that story ended.
How will I end?

So many tears – still here
choking at my life.

I hoped to shed them along
and emerge strong and shining.

But I am still here
in this dark place.
Scared.

I am waving my hand and calling
            to you.
I have told millions of jokes.
I have kept you laughing.

But you never caught my tears.
Unless you do, I will die.
Will you notice if I die?

Will you remember me smiling
            or not at all?

My tears will not be here
            for a hundred years.

I will wash away with them.
Unless you put out your hand
            and catch them.

I don't want to die – catch them

Hide

My Most Precious Lord and Saviour,
is this the face of suffering?
my face –
his face –

hide this face
for it is defiled
and despised.
It is the Lord's,
the face of dark.

See how these other paler faces
turn away
from your dark
into their own.

Hide this face.
It is mine.
It is his.

Living his passion
is not beautiful,
it is defiled
and despised.

See these dim figures
turn away in horror
from his
from yours.

Hide my wounds
in yours
deep and dark and bloody
for yours is the only dark

that is good
that is rest
that is light.

This face
Mine –
his.

My Dark Saviour,
drape your suffering
over mine
that I might lose all light
in your dark
and
for one brief eternity

Rest.

Woo the Woe

Woo my heart freely
for it is full of woe.
Woe   Woe   Woe
deep and darkly mine.

Woo my heart freely,
my Savior and my Lord.
Grief, Sorrow are familiar
but not friends
(not enemies either) –
just dark companions
on the low road.

Woo my heart freely,
Beautiful Savior,
I am alone with you.
No one else need know
how much we are in love.

To My Jesus,

O Sweet Recompense

O Sweet Recompense
your bloody cross strong
its aching crossbeams
holding the weight of the world.

O Sweet Recompense
the haunting beautiful terror
of your torn and suffering limbs
you are the nothingness point
where we all begin
where we all end.

O Sweet Recompense
you dear cross of Christ
your tortured form raises me
                  to the heavens
      and spreads me deep and wide among the pilgrims.
I suffer with you
          for you
               through you.
You have crucified me.

O Sweet Recompense!

The Darkening Eye

Walking an ordinary street
in full ordinary sunlight
brushing by anonymous human forms
something shoves you down
clangs shut, rings
affirmative and metallic.

You know tragedy
straight on –
a full mirror shattering
a speckle of blood in a tiny vein
       behind the retina
throbs and thickens
clots and clogs, pulls the heavy
       lidded cover over.

The darkening eye is one mercy
you can live
and even this straight street
you walked today
can be someone else's, not yours
the black hole you dwell in
is simply an eye unopened
air not breathed.

You lie deep in the dark
a small curled form
you made it
somehow you survived
you know tragedy straight on
and you live
you live
unopened.

Section Three:

In a Time of Peace

God Is an Italian

Lord, what pizzazz!
Your broad warm creased
Pizza-loaded-with-everything face
grins wide and benign
tosses this doughy world
into wildly spinning space
as one massive fleshy finger
holds steady at its axis
and then nonchalantly falls asleep
in the oven's warmth.

Faith

Faith is
in not having
not touching
not seeing.

***

Faith is
in sightless seeing
untouched touching
silent loving.

***

Faith is only found
when needed
only real
when used
until then
it is a seed
waiting to burst
forth into
living hope.

Teach Me, Jesus

Teach me, Jesus –
I am a poor student,
I have to learn the same things
        over and over again
and each time they seem new, deeper,
        harder to learn.

Teach me, Jesus –
        sometimes I am a precocious student –
I think, ponder heavy thoughts,
I get in over my head,
I try too hard, get nervous,
        overanxious,
and give up in despair.

Teach me, Jesus –
        but let your lessons
be leavened with humor
and shove me out of your church
when I have prayed overlong.

Teach me, Jesus –
I need your depth and your lightness.
Take me away from abstractions
and give me a parable.
Return me to the fisherman and farmer,
anchor my roots in the dark earth,
and carry me in the silver sea.

Teach me how you loved.
Let me know the poor, the dirty, the slow,
        the troubled.
Let me know the clean, the intelligent,
        the well-dressed, the smug.

Let me know them equally,
      draw no distinctions,
      form no judgments.

If there are judgments to be made,
      success or failure meted out,
      let them be yours.

Rabbi, Great Teacher, teach me.

Dancing through the Healing

Small movements
      under your brooding spirit
strong in fragility
trembling – smiling
losing
      losing still more
confident – serene
shaking hollow vessel
fearing the final shattering
seeming so imminent
      strained to the ultimate
going on past it
      following through the healing
      dancing through the healing
my body stumbles
seeming to weaken
my spirit remains strong
a contradiction, the hidden paradox
fluttering, moving, small movements
under your brooding spirit
      dancing
           through
               the healing.

My Sanctuary

My sanctuary

a cooled line
      held tight

against rough round space.

Precisely sun-spotted
dappled in deep shadow
an oriental teapot
plays host to sheer draperies
the polished wood, sweet with wax
intersects the walls, winter white and smooth.

My sanctuary,
my space defined
and held in
      by hard lines
released by billowy light
a place of contradictions
      reconciled
a cooled line
      held tight
against my round space.

Let Me Play with You, Jesus

Let me play with you, Jesus,
you are so much fun.
This is our little secret –
we are playing in Jesus' park,
we are playing in the graveyard.

It is so peaceful here,
the trees are greenly gently
swaying with our bodies.
We are dancing.
You are happy again.

Let me play with you, Jesus,
I love you so.
You glow with deep burnished beauty.
I run and hop among the tombstones –
I am playing with your death,
I am loving it, holding it, making it light.

You are my Savior.
You are playing with me, Jesus.
Beautiful Child,
we touch, we touch,
we admire the exquisite beauty we are.

Let me play with you, Jesus,
you are too serious.
Let me make you laugh,
let me take you away from the tomb
of the tabernacle
and the coldness of the altar
– the serious words of the priests.

Let me play with you, Jesus,

you are too sad.
I want to make you laugh.
Let me play with you, Jesus,
I love you.
Do not be cold,
do not be afraid of Death,
the cold.

Where There Are Wounds

Where there are wounds
we need words.

So often there are only
those deadly bloodless wounds
denied words, denied bloody life.

Dried, seemingly lifeless wounds –
we choose to shove them down,
smile bravely, so hideously brave.

They rise up again.
It is inevitable.
Red and snarling
menaces of hate, hurt
entangling our lives.

Now the words are here.
He speaks them.
His words are streaming, flowing
        over me, over my wounds.

Now there is deeper pain,
the hurt, the terror, the betrayal
felt as it was before
by an innocent child.

No longer shoved down
it rises in all its hate and hurt.
I keep walking.
I must.

His words continue to flow
over me, over my wounds.
I trust in him.
I have no one else.

Now he is easing the memory, the fear,
the pain.
Each day is a gradual easing away
as peace enters in.

Where there were wounds
he brought words –

he brought himself.

To Ann,

Be

Be
in the heat of the day
in the still of the night.

Be
as cities tumble
and buildings crumble
people running in ever-widening circles.

Pause.
Stop.
And be.

Be to yourself
a mighty fortress
admitting only those
      who build
      not destroy
as a mighty tree
gains strength from nature.

Be
Absorb the nutrients of the soil
toss your leaves in the sunshine
let the rain soak deep into dark roots.

Be, my child,
as I am.
Do not allow
everyone into your realm.
Treasure yourself
yet be.

Be open to the sky
turning over its long days
        into long nights
and again into days.
Open to the passing cloud
        or twig
        or branch.
Open to the heart
seeking yours.
Open to the widest galaxies
and the smallest creatures.

Be, my child.
Live.
Love.
And Be.

Free Floating

Free floating
    in a time of peace
        drifting in and out
            of timelessness
touching the eternal
    with recurrent reverent breaths
        passing on
        to the solid flesh
        of humanity
        quivering fingers
        hover over the translucence
            of loved ones.
How glorious they are
in their humanness
    how eternal
    and timeless
    integral grained depth
    of swirling skin surface
        the forms of him
        hovering on the horizon.

The Glorious Presence
Serene Silvered Majesty
    reclines on the flesh
        free floating
            in recurrent breaths
                through days
        permeated with golden hues
    transformed into the robes of flesh
    a loving translucence
        free floating
encompassing the smallest
    and the largest
        serenely passing over

and living within
this compact luminous universe
this glorious transcendent immanence
free floating
past and over and beyond
many days turning over
into many nights and again
season after season
breathing in and out
germinating slowly growing flourishing
in abundance
then slow decline
as the years become
minutes
as we drift
free floating
into Eternity.

Grey Buddha

My cat
sits on my poems
like the grey wise
Buddha she is
with her white apron
and inexplicable eyes.

She moves when I pull them out
from under her –
knowing my force and realm
are outside her
she will accommodate
like a woman
always accommodating
like a poet
moving with the wind.

How good to move with the wind
to let it blow across
the plane of my features
and carve God's impression there.

I am a supremely rational being
and I believe in a supremely
rational God
who showed very good sense
when he made me
a poet
and provided a grey cat
to sit on my poems.

Some of Us

Some of us are born
with a meaning in our mouths.

I was born with a concept
wafer-like on my tongue
and he issued forth
carefully executed
oily with knowledge.

He seeks precision,
integrated parts.
He originates,
        delegates,
            follows through.

A leader, first-born,
his name pronounces itself.

Dear Friend

Dear Friend, we can hear the music now.
You are bringing the colors
and I am bringing the words
and someone else is here too
though he is indistinct
and strangely burdened.

I do not think
we will die
just yet
but let us hold each other's hand
as we travel
through the heaviness.

Come, let us look for him in the dawn
before the world knows our movements.

How good you are

If There Is Hope

If there is hope here
(and there is),
it is of a different species or genre
than yesterday's vapor trail.

It rises up green and pushy,
splits the earth even now
in the midst of winter.
The heart rocks a bit, then stretches
and lets out a note:
        Hope.
Come now – push free – stretch –
show your stuff – strut a little.

Bring me a flower today –
speak to me of a difference –
a day grown new
a higher sky
a light meeting the eye
and more – .

If there is hope here
(and there is),
it won't be coaxed, cajoled,
or sent invitations.
It whispers to me of a promise – .

Hope – I won't cling to you,
demand of you,
or make plans for you
but simply fly
like tomorrow's balloon
into a new space.

Looking for Jesus

The Lord warns me
not to peer around corners
and I no longer do
as in years past

when I watched the skies
for signs and portents,
counted my tea leaves
and arranged my chairs and tables
to be ready to receive him
whom I longed for
in all his splendor.

All this ended only in disappointment
and distress – so I took my clever intellect
and precise imaginings and shelved them,
high up, where I could never go again.

Now I no longer peek around corners
or hint of profound secrets
and Jesus speaks to me very simply now –
sometimes in my garage, walking to the car,
sometimes while washing dishes, making a bed,
or turning off a light.

I cannot explain it, except to say that
Jesus does not wish to be pursued intently.
He is not a prize to be won
by dint of hard labor.

Rather he likes to be invited in –
into our celebrations and our sorrows –
into our family gatherings and our solitude –
into the midst of the most ordinary day – .

Let him take a seat in your kitchen
and while you work he will become
a friend,
a companion,
a man on a journey.

And,
Blessed be God,
he will take you
                with him.

To Daddy,

When My Hands Grow Stronger

Someday
when my hands grow stronger
I will gather all those I love
into soft folds around my body
and hold them.

And then –
I will turn their faces
toward the light
so they may see
their beauty
and love
each other.

Somedays

Somedays
permeated by drizzle
wet fog and steamy panes
wrap me in a boggy blanket.

I do not move
except for slight stirrings
of tired muscles
and weighted breast.

These days have
a sweetness,
a secret sweetness,
for others resist
the weary dreary drizzle

while I lap at it
like a hazy grey kitten
sweet curled laps
of a grainy pink tongue.

I stir in the shadows
then nuzzle down deeper
into the down of the day
of a dripping, lovely
dripping day
softly spending itself
into the quietness
of my being.

A Letter Home

I wrote home today
in my mind:
"The wildflowers give me much pleasure."

and then fell silent
my thoughts heavy and slow

like a tree bending low
over the water
leaves close-spaced, airless,
never sees, never reflects
on its reflection,

so my mind
thick with silence
slows – then stops
something gives out
into something better.

Maybe this poem was written
by a small girl of ten
holding an oak leaf on her palm
years ago
in her backyard.

Surely it is not I
slow with summer and an older ease
someone younger maybe
persists in struggling to find a word
for this –

While I am content to write home
in my mind:
"The wildflowers give me much pleasure."

The best years wait.

To Edward,

Seeing You

Seeing you is
>seeing the clouds
>white – windswept – free.

Touching you is
>touching the earth
>deep – dark – moist.

Kissing you is
>losing the earth, the clouds
>spinning in darkest space.

Loving you is
>loving all men, all women
>in one crushing embrace.

Being with you
>I am
>closest to God
>and loving you
>I love him.

To Edward,

Time Lapse

You are blurred, darkened
I am incisive, light.
You meander
I pierce.
Your petals open slowly
Mine burst forth impulsively.
You blunder upon the same treasure
I lunge into.
We share this treasure
in slow dark obscurity
and quick incisive light.
Turning it over
in each other's time lapse
we fold inward
without movement.

I Have a Memory, Some Have a Dream

I have a memory
half-formed, whispering,
it bids me into a new space,
a new time, an occasion even
      set apart.

I have a memory of here,
this future now present
across the smooth white table
      of today.

Some have a dream,
of which I express no need,
preferring this,
this half-formed presence,
this breathing,
      these lips

forming vowels, consonants, meanings
exchanged in space and time and silence
where memory breathes and grows
      and breathes and grows.

We meet today across this smooth white table
our minds submerged and transfixed:
      A round open space
      a moon almost full
      a smooth water of light
      a shimmering on lifted trees.

We have a memory, no dream,
of form and breath and space.
Maybe, yes, maybe,
it is us we met today
in this present space of yesterday –
      a memory, maybe, of tomorrow.

My Word

My word, now simpler.
My note, now lower.
My sound, now sweeter.
My heart, now winged.
My soul, now submerged.

My space, limitless and secure.
My form, light – clear.
My path, unknown – shining.
My glory, certain.
My praise, unending.

Section Four:

Wise Child

Wise Child

What is a wise child?

Sensual, sensitive, wise and gifted is this child.
She has regained her innocence, not so much lost
as undiscovered.

Now she can lie and gaze at the sky for hours with
no need of books or music.

When she plays, she plays with pursed-mouth concentration,
until she tires of it and throws it aside.

When she works, she works fast and hard to get it done
well and get it done quickly.

When she listens, she is completely passive as the sound
gathers meaning, as the person becomes known and loved.

When she touches, she touches lightly and her whole
body throbs at its own recognition.

When she loves, she is utterly vulnerable and dependent.
She cannot hide her needs or her desire to please.

Her innocence protects her.
She is a wise child.

She will never be more or less than this.

A Self-Conscious Affliction

I am a poet
a self-conscious affliction.
My eyes blink shutterlike
singling out, superimposing
dark on light, curve on straight.

My line cast out
in a wide circle
a slow whirring curving arc
then a sure plummet
into
as a blue dragonfly zips past
wide dark pupils
and is gone.

I record every image
in casual precision
even sprawled artistically across a warm body
I am conscious of the placement
of my hands on the face, the limbs
and raging release is replaced
by the image of an ivory calf
suspended over dark buttocks.

It Remembers Everything

Lying wound
　by this curved wand of sleep

I breathe inaudibly
　the sucking warm sea air

While my curled forming suspends
　heavily in liquid space

And a dream rolls out its significance
　far into the dawn.

The silence so weighty, so thickened
　only one syllable slips through

To bubble up, nudging the closed limbs,
　clenched fists, sealed lips

Breaking the brittle spittle film,
　loosing the low rolling mouth sound

Penetrating the infant wet skin,
　It saturates the consciousness.

I wake from babyhood
one husky word in my throat
and uncurl my close warmth
into the blank stare of the sun.

The word preceded then
as it does now
it issues forth
　　from the seawater of my womb
to push me into a gray world
　　of alien silence.

My word is still here
lodged somewhere

between my heart and throat
and pulses like the womb.

It remembers everything.

The Thrush

The thrush rests in a bush
  secret little soft
My mind holds a bush
  and thrush brown slurred
The lobed leaf and feathered bush…
Secret little thing
Do not move
  In my mind.

This Small Fallen Circle

Pre-dawn darkness
a vague autumn presence
dark gold – heavy
I lie crumpled and barely conscious
to softened air, flowing blood
hair spread in a flower of warmth.

This semi-state enters
into floating colors
that flurrying, scurrying, scud
like fragments, curling
gold and rust scraps
tossed up in a warm October rain.

Pre-dawn darkness
I strain into it, one knee
pressed into the sheets
one mind floating free behind filmy eyelids
the hair sensuous and gold
above a langorous curving form.

This suspended life –
Here I am – open
to the lidded mind
closed to the striving form
here in pre-dawn autumn
the womb's webby water
laps at my limbs
while my mind is being formed
by gold fragments
filtering in on my mother's last mood.

Loomy force in the wind
the fertile earth

I dropped into, decomposes
beneath my tucked form,
fawn fragile,
in my small fallen circle

the arc I traversed yesterday
a dim meaning in my form
yet this mind holds womb water
hangs suspended
in the pre-dawn darkness
of another age.

You, Lovey

A small bubble
spittle-like
formed in cool consciousness
by the mouth mind,

You, Lovey,

Fragile and soap slippery
with a smooth cold cream touch
                on my moony mind
        surface
                drift lazily upward
                        shimmer light
        a pinkly lavender concoction
                sugary spun
                        spittle bubble,

        You, Lovey.

The Poet

Ideas plop in her lap
plump black olives
split – revealing meaty innards.

She tries to push them away
tired of their barrage
Plop – another one, this one an apple
clutches at her skirt.

She is resigned to this
ripe plopping
a poet must accommodate nature
she cannot disregard the fruit
whether bitter or sweet,
          full or shriveled
they belong here
in her lap, at her skirt
and she uses them
to feed circular polished rhythms
into straight hidebound minds.

A poet grows tired
of making use
          of tree limbs
                    a passing cloud
                              and red wheelbarrows
a poet grows tired
even in her sleep
          images shove and crowd
her shutter mind clicks and records
without her permission.

She is a victim
of strange forces
and willingly goes under.

Her widescreen mind
finds the technicolor world
startling and razor-edged.

Take what she gives you
if you can find the time
for she only creates
        to give it away
and winter is hiding
in the apple blossom.

Woman to Woman

Still you restrain a wing
        bend in a forearm

Curve the eyelash down

Denigrate the round lip.

Still you perform your cosmetic surgery
        every day

Slicing off your link
        with the rest of us

Insisting on a predominance of form
        over sensibility.

And if we should need you

You would present
        the needed implement

As if it were
        yourself.

The Darkening Eye

Walking an ordinary street
in full ordinary sunlight
brushing by anonymous human forms
something shoves you down
clangs shut, rings
affirmative and metallic.

You know tragedy
straight on –
a full mirror shattering
a speckle of blood in a tiny vein
        behind the retina
throbs and thickens
clots and clogs, pulls the heavy
        lidded cover over.

The darkening eye is one mercy
you can live
and even this straight street
you walked today
can be someone else's, not yours
the black hole you dwell in
is simply an eye unopened
air not breathed.

You lie deep in the dark
a small curled form
you made it
somehow you survived
you know tragedy straight on
and you live
you live
unopened.

Without Cloy

I am so damn bitter
and so damn sweet
without cloy
that my mouth puckers and sucks
and swallows all things.

I put the world in it and
no one knows
cause my teeth
are so damn friendly
that they are comfortable
while I chew on them.

God, who is this strange being
that can eat and leave whole?
while sucking and grinding
appears to be only rosy puckeriness
over fragile China.

She is not insidious.
She is not a monster.

She just is.
And she eats.

Normal Day

Make me a poet
of the every day
for the day contains
all things.

Let the day slide past
into home, a slow glide
containing the grace and form
I yearn for
in this abrupt world
of interrupted pauses
and hasty gulps
a slow slide of a day
beginning with the slow slide
of awakening
coasting downhill
into the earthly garden
of delights
nibbling there
a gray velveteen rabbit
among the cabbages.

Aaron – Bringer of Light

Five years old, almost six
a golden pineapple chunk boy
he watches me with quiet concern
drinking water from the tap,
then shakes his head firmly at me,
this is not good –

"From now on," he says, "you must drink only
mountain water, only mountain water."
Yes, Aaron, whatever you say, Aaron.

Nourish me, golden ray
with your cool sunshine
delicate, fine-veined, sun-filtered child.

We love each other.
We think we are grand.

You are cool, you are wonder,
You are a finely-tuned instrument
at perfect pitch.

Roll out your soft music for me.

The Body Speaks

I am your fleshiness,
I put meat on your bones
thickness to your sinew
and beef stew mounds
      of potato and carrot.

I am your fleshiness
      filling up your chinks
even my thin stalk of nose
      inhales the grape arbor
my eyes grasp its twisty tangled
      grapey globule
now purple roundly sweet
colors and forms your nowhere.
If my tongue dares to snake
      into that same grape arbor
it too recoils in delight
savoring juice purple.

My fingers can go on
forgetting fruit
exploring new fleshiness,
      new land masses
flowing free in dark rivers
      of pleasure.

Must I continue?
Your body is ageless
it has a tradition of dignity
only debased by ignorance.

Do not disdain it
in favor of amorphous concepts
there is fleshiness
          in spirit
and spirit
          in fleshiness.

If you cannot value me
You will be nothing
but a wisp of flame
in a fast approaching storm.

Flesh too has immortality
even as it falls away.
Treasure me, touch me, feed me,
lay me out in sun and shadow
when your spirit comes out to play
I will romp with it.

I am your fleshiness.
Hear me.

Wild Sweet Innocence

Your cool coiled passion
       lies intent
while innocent, brave
       I enter deeper
           deeper than before
              into your closed domain
feeling in your drawn eyes
       sad territorial fear
I draw back afraid,
       no longer young –

Waiting outside your dark line
       a glimmer
           a silver shadow
              womanly presence
                 stirring
     waiting
       waiting

sensing
    the
       whole fury
the rustling increases
          increases
I grow older, sweeter, more innocent
I sense your coiled stillness
I wait
      I wait
    a silver streak of pain
         across your dark bed of fury.

My Body Was Wise

While my brain danced its frenzied dance,
probed assembled,
      probed assembled
danced again,

My body was wise.

While my brain shriveled and starved,
      shrunken gaping skull
feared its own death,

My body was wise.

Round White Milky. The Moon.
It took the Penis, it took the Food, it chewed
and even when it did not eat,

My body was wise.

I am quieting my brain
I am lengthening the silences
better left unspoken, unasked.

Strong Body, Strong Child, growing quietly
strong and full into primitive womanhood,
it lies on the earth.

Now my brain is quieting
Now the silence is white and milky
Now the moon shimmers on the rippling trees.
Now it is over.

You Probably Think Me

You probably think me
an Incurable Romantic
but I can go to the supermarket
like anyone else
though my elephant
sometimes gives me trouble
over the meat counter.

A Walk in Three Parts

I.
The trees arched
        with gold sharped leaves –

In the bitter air
I hear the sounds of children
        coming grouped
In hard brown bodies
their faces wide open
flashing.

Yet I turn the page and walk on –

II.
Now the street sags
        with dusty limbs
        and I see a child alone
        his face a brown leaf
        fluttering.

III.
Maybe in November
when bare limbs cease to signify
I will see more
than uneasy trees
        a wandering leaf –

And yet those children are not enough
All I see are those trees
        arched and fluttering

Something goes wrong
in October.

To Lorri,

Young Bi-Centennial Woman

Seventeen years in 1976.

Cancer

Her stay shortened and saddened
An ethereal creature with coffee-colored eyes
In this year of Our Lord 1976
Dear Bi-Centennial Young
We know you so well.
We see your shining
Young and American
Brimming, daisy-fresh, life
overflows into your eyes
your laughter rings with the liberty bell.

Your stay may be shortened
those woeful frowning doctors tell us
How little they know!
You have traveled so far,
my little one,
many miles in a step,
and taken us with you.

We will live the next 100 years for you
and remember your brimming laughter,
when it is silenced.

O Young Bi-Centennial Woman,
living free in this vast country
it seems we must lose you
as we are losing this summer of our lives
and moving gently into middle age
Hushed by the remembrance of
        your youth
        your shining
        your freshness

Quiet laughing one
Bi-Centennial Woman
Must we say good-bye
Beautiful Child of America

To Edward,

Just the Other Day

The air smells of rain today
as it did yesterday
when we visited and touched.

I carried your sadness away with me
                in my hands
and laid it under the kitten on the porch.

She purred over it
                pawed it a bit
liked your sadness
(as I do)
and settled down over it
like a pearl gray cloud.

When I retrieved your sadness
                some time later
it was much lighter
no longer black
but pearl gray

I took the little remaining
and tucked it under my pillow.
That night your dense dark body
moved in slow motion
                through brooding dreams.

When I awoke
I lifted my pillow
and found a fluted seashell
strung around my neck.

Now everyone remarks
at its delicate form
and I say, Yes,
a friend gave it to me
just the other day
when the air smelled of rain.

Cloud Amour

Cloud Amour
        lazy lavender breath
flown, sown inward
                and released –
shot through vapor
                    obscuring a dim earth
                        round and remote.

Cloud Amour
        clearly formless
and replete in silver harvests
                of unknown moons
spinning sparse in space
            permeating
                    penetrates
world layers
        wound round and remote,
Climbs
        and surmounts
                dark form, limbs, mass
                    voiceless sound
                        animal silence.

Cloud Amour
breath issuing mildly lavender
        silver moon transpiring
                into streaming clarity
                    streaking infinite space

flown inward
        and released
over a lost earth
        spinning round and remote
through lazy lavender breath
                issuing
                    Cloud Amour.

Section Five:

Behind My Curtain

Behind My Curtain

The rain came today
at dawn
behind my curtain
a gentle influence
a whisper.

I woke
to soft robes
a white coffee cup
an absence of desire.

The rain came today
and remains
an interminable day
a backdrop
to a mood.

I wait
alone and timeless
and the rain drops
and continues
to drop.

Soft words
falling
into the earth
a presence of peace
behind my curtains
a whisper.

Dance Brother, Dance Sister

Weep your tears
    in my free white space

Shout your joy
    in my hollow silence

I am emptied to receive
    all you are

And free enough to live
    within my boundaries
    and yours,

Our stillness moves
    in the timeless rhythm
      we share

And we dance, dance
    in each other's darkness
      each other's light.

My Brothers, My Sisters
    My space, my silence
    is yours,

My darkness speaks of light,
    My light speaks of dark
      My flesh speaks of your flesh,

Dance Brother
    Dance Sister

Our stillness moves
    in the timeless rhythm
      we share.

Vision Unclaimed

The net draped to dry
in the sun
white, torn, bleached
like my sight caught up
in waiting
while the wind shifts gentle
with summer and untroubled memories.

Eyes deeper and rested
blue with waiting
and nothing else.
Satisfied with pale washes
and a few grapes.

Maybe this evening
will bring
deeper tones, defined structures
vowels and consonants held up to the sky
a scene complete
with a doorway even
or maybe a window is enough,
until then
       a casual certain air
       a light tip of the tongue
       a grape
       a finger or two
       curled and loose,

Not reckoning with weather
only change
and that internal and recollected
       to that tiny cornea
       that seed
       that curled bud
       that vision
         unclaimed.

Trying to Define the Indefinable

Poetry is the intellectualism of the heart
a university without rooms
a scattering of students
in dark obscure corners

      ***

Poetry is the heart's answer
to the word-weary mind
the dreamless sleep
the silent question.

      ***

Poetry drifts in
on a broken flight of pain
and fastens to the heart
a winged promise.

Let Me

Let me be your marigold
    small sturdy and golden

Let me run unbridled through your wilderness
    tossing tumbleweeds into tomorrow

Let me savour the day like a plump golden apple
    held against innocent white teeth

Let me fly whimsical red balloons
    to crash against the sun

Let me capture you in a word and roll that word
    over and over and over
    tumbling over my tongue
    in the warm dark hollows

Let me fold your curve of neck into mine
    so you won't seep out and run down
    and away from me

Let me be the woman I am becoming
    and love the little child in me.

Let me hold you here
    whatever way you wish.

Some Are Wild – Some Are Cultivated

I stroll through the woods
seeing dead birds, singing birds
moss green water, clear water
tiny moist pink flowers,
fallen dried curled leaves
something is very wild
something rough and ready
something to get your teeth into.

I stroll directly through these woods
to see a man oiling his lawnmower
children playing ball
a dog yapping happily
something is very tame here
something smooth and used
something to be comfortable with.

Some are wild – some are cultivated
You are both –
      Let me stroll
            through your mind.

To Edward,

Nightingale

You never bring flowers
blossoms of any sort
instead –
long artist hands
large, dark, tips flattened
smoothed
from years of oil.

Bring me your hands
and place them here –
in my light hair
hold them that way
you do
hovering and near
as light as a wing
brush against me
like a dark bird
songless and sad
and touch my cheek
my eyes
my lips
before you drift away.

You are a sad song
I have sung, sweet and soft
and I will not leave you
there
alone and mute
without wings –
without words –

Take my song, my words –
Be my nightingale of sorrow
singing bird
with rainbows
 on your wings.

Jerusalem, O Jerusalem!

You are an enclosed garden
a paradise secure
flesh and bone of ordered grace
a comeliness without allure.

Your robe is always white
your flesh sweet and dry
Your warm hair falls brown
and free to the neck
unencumbered by brain or pin.

You walk in beauty
like an evening hush
Your paradise all green and gold.

Your mind fertile
warm, tropical and full
with rare fruits.

You breathe a filmy breeze
through young trees
Your feet slender as willow leaves.

Your notes silver green and light
you dream sunlight and motion
without thought.

All is ease and order
for you are the Lord's
and He fastens you
like a jewel to His breast
and strides great strides
across the desert.

Jerusalem, O Jerusalem!

Watch with me
for yet another hour
that I might wake
to your whispering breath
and touch your rose sky

with a Word.

Make Use

Make use – make use
The world revolves repeating
make use make use.

Better the expanse
Better the sky
Better the nothingness
of holes in the dark night
bringing tomorrows
of wonder.

A Plenitude

If I could immerse
a day
I would –
dropped through heavy liquid
warmed muted softened
a pebble of silence
a quiet pool
a plenitude of peace.

Self Self

Sisters, brothers call it home
I regard it a piece of resistance
a strangeness
a neighborhood pretend
set down far back
a childhood remembered
and let loose
relinquished

choosing this older place
this present sense
this half lifetime remaining
for something more foreign and older than I
the potter's wheel
wandering hieroglyphics

leaving behind guarded yards
pictures on the mantle
lilacs, white curtains
a bedroom.

Come link me over
onto a new peninsula
a predominance
a cliff

Come with me now
   Self
   Self
found here in this kinder air
this outjutting
this peninsula
this outspace

soon you will perceive an island
remote
and leave this figure
without haste
crossing over vast landholdings
toward a round living
a reverie of green space
among the waters
      Self
      Self.

Choices

We make arbitrary choices
about non-arbitrary matters,
I choose burial
the moldering earth, a natural habitat
containing rank living
systematic dying.

You choose fire
a violent consuming
swifter and purer
a very satisfactory removal
lifting you cleanly
into drifting currents.

This suits us.
We have some control
over the inevitable
as we creep forward
into my squatter's rights
your flight regulations
our non-choice
leading to a choice.

Dialogue on the Appropriate

Comment: "That is totally inappropriate."

Reply: "Yes, I am a human being and that in itself
　　　is totally inappropriate."

　　　***

Comment: "By not being appropriate, you are inflicting
　　　violence on my appropriateness."

Reply: "If you let my appropriate live, we can both
　　　share an appropriate existence."

　　　***

"I am becoming so inappropriate by writing about
appropriateness!"

What If

What if every bit of alive
had a mind?

What is each grass blade
felt the wind,
knew the dirt,
thought about the sky?

How horrible to think of trees thinking,
asking questions
of a blank sky.

How noisy our universe could be
with a mind in each bit
of green.

Love's Vague Finger

Love's vague finger points
to connections never made
And our tired boxcars
couplings linked
carry the everyday
into the commonplace.

A Serious Person

A serious person
has time enough
a relentless tickertape
programs his day:

      7 hours of serious
      5 hours of trivial
      4 hours of mindless.

Then he lapses
into 8 hours of sleep
containing:

      3 hours of technicolor dreams
      3 hours of a dark cavern
      2 hours of snoring and twitching.

A serious person
can go on like this
for years
till he throws
it all over
for 24 hours of dead.

My Dear William

Someday I will look
deeply into your eyes,
lovingly clasp your hand,
and say,
"And how are you, my dear William?"
And you will look at me
thinking
this tragic dame
is one classy broad.
And I will say:
Yes, Bogie always
thought so
though he kicked me
around a bit.

Void

The gray void of day rains
misted minds and drabbed eyes.

We wake, hands clutching
color images garnered from sleep fields.

We flow, blanched slivers of men
passive driftwood changing with the current.

We drift
        unmoved.

Ha!

I like my lumpy lard
I like children laughing at my fatness
and chortling with them.

I enjoy being injured
and carrying this lumbrous burden in clumsy gropings.
I enjoy being laughable.
I am a joke.
Laugh with me,
Do not look at my beauty, do not admire me.

Laugh at me – Ha! Ha!
I am funny.
I am a funny creature.
I am laughing.
I am clumsy, groping, funny,
Laugh with me –

Ha.

Voice Enough

I never speak of the wind.
It has voice enough
for multitudes.
My guarded enclosure
offers a silence, a vigilance
ears turned away from its mouth
its coarse breathing
its noise.

I never speak of the wind.
It speaks of me
turning up wings
white tips
clouds furrowed and seeded
small shadowed creatures
skirmishing, frightened
tiny bright eyes.

I turn and head into it
heedless and indifferent
my flesh itself an obstacle
not seeing the newspaper tossed up,
the seagull of city streets,
turning away from worn threads
and squalor –
I head into it.

Someday I will call to it
bid it
will it come –
to sweep bare the snow,
a new place,
a square of freshness
a tablecloth of grace
until then

I never speak of the wind,
It has voice enough
for multitudes.

Passages

Making my way
I dip and slip over
into another river reverie
drowsy, dusted with time
warm with pastel memories
enough to paint a skyline
on today's edge.

Reminiscing becomes richer
as the years slip by
and now, without rudder or anchor,
I cease to plan or consult
timetables.
I simply find the pulse of the river
and place my body beside it
and breathe with it.

I live on this particular slant of sun
this bit of crumbling earth
this dusty, beclouded room
of mind and imaginings
is all I know
and not much more.

Ah, the simplicity of being young
while being old
of not needing
more than a little color
a little sun
a brief touching.

Should you see me
for just one shimmering second
I can only wave hello
and call – it is good here

and eternity surely must be fine.

Section Six:

Wiser Now

Centerhold

Recoiled action
energy line flung out
reeling in
a slow whirring arc
line coiling, winding circle
upon circle
rolling back upon itself
smaller and smaller
closes its strict confines
dark and tight
small smooth pebble
black and stony
centerhold –
Self

On Faith

You cannot enjoy the Absolute like an ice cream cone.

    ***

Complete surrender is probably
not possible in this life. Only
Jesus can fully surrender to the Father.
Perhaps if we place our hearts and
wills inside Jesus, he can
take possession of us and surrender
us to the Father. This requires
great courage but Jesus has enough
for all of us.

    ***

Everything I have is here.
Everything I am is here.
Everything I need is here.
Sweet Enclosure.

    ***

Blest, O Lord,
is the silence
that surrounds and envelopes
but especially the silence
of my center.

    ***

Jesus, Saviour
my power
my footing
sheer majesty
mountain of certainty
defying the elements
together
partners
in this adventure
chosen
blest
given over
to a newly
birthed life.

***

***

He comes in
humility and peace
and settles down
upon us just
where trust begins
to grow with
ever-increasing strength.

***

To love with fervor
a God who
reveals himself
is a very great grace
but greater still
is to love
in dryness a God
who seems absent.
The will responds
to hidden
promptings and all
that is necessary
is accomplished.
Glory to God in
his hiddenness!

***

Wherever peace
abides, he is.

***

"To know as I am known" – what
a bold prayer!
Does he promise this, too?

***

Becoming one's self necessarily involves
pain. Joy follows but it begins
and travels through pain.

***

Martyrdom takes place on an
almost daily level when we have
surrendered self to the Godhead.

***

His grace is
flowing golden
light over the
darkness of pain
and suffering.
A dark world trembles
at his touch.

***

To love my God
is my all and my
everything. O Jesus,
if only my intentions
were as pure as
I profess! Such a great
discrepancy between
the truth we believe
and the falsehood
of our thoughts and
actions.

***

Finding my way
through the intricacies
of the moment,
I sometimes glimpse
the vast simplicity
of eternity.

***

"My soul clings
to you; your right
hand holds me fast."

***

It seems I
very much lack
a firm trust and
hope though God
has never disappointed
me and always provides
the best of care. To be human
is to forget and to
fear. I ask for
the grace to remember
and from that
remembrance,
hope.

***

An exile here
but what a
glorious homeland!

**

None of us live
without God because
none of us live
without sunlight.

**

To remember to
remember is a
living hope.

**

The Mother of God
touches my words
with her grandeur.

**

Sometimes I find pious people
nauseating. They
give God a bad
reputation.

**

To love God with all
your mind, all your
heart, and all your
strength is all
that is necessary.

***

        ***

God can be glimpsed
in the spaces
between and around
the words of our
prayers more than in the
words themselves.

        ***

Obedience asks us
to wait in a darkness that
our faith knows God
will eventually pierce
with his light. Jesus does
not operate on a
timetable of our own
making.

        ***

We are to carry
our crosses, not
compare them. No
one really knows
what suffering
another is bearing.
It is a solitary
agreement between
the pilgrim and his
God.

***

If I seek answers,
it means I am
wallowing in anxiety
and looking for a
cure. Jesus
gives progress notes
that inch me along
the path he has
chosen for me.

***

My heart yearns for
a certainty my mind
cannot find. (Jesus
gives it – I do
not find it.)

***

130

You cannot strain to
obtain God's wisdom
because too much
"you" is in the
striving. Once you
are emptied of
"youness," he will come.
Do not fear emptiness.
Be patient.
At first you will be scared.
Later you will be
sacred.

***

My pain, my suffering, is not
beautiful but if I live it
out in truth with loving
surrender it transforms itself
into the beautiful.

***

Waiting and listening.

***

Just waiting.

On the Poet

Poetry is the intellectualism of the heart
a university without rooms
a scattering of students
in dark obscure corners.

***

Poetry is the heart's answer
to the word-weary mind
the dreamless sleep
the silent question.

***

I am a child
not of impulse
but of listening
and quiet movement.

***

My mind never ceases
to amaze me
with its
straight convolutions.

***

I'm so diffuse
that I concentrate
on the everything.

***

"You are an
incomprehensible
word in the
poetry you live."

***

I spend my time
patiently endeavoring
to catch up
with myself
and put a stop to it
immediately.

***

Why do I have
to remind my body
to move
when my mind keeps moving
on its own?

***

My mind sometimes
justifies its existence
in the first hour of the morning
and sleeps away
the rest of the day.

***

I must simply live myself.

***

To know our limitations
is simply
to define our abilities.

***

Whenever I am good, I surprise myself.

***

Punctuation is awfully loose
these days but then –
who isn't?

On Love

To love and to be loved –
how we complicate the simplicity of it all!
Is there no end to our foolishness?

***

To find your mid-section is my ideal
as you keep presenting
relentlessly presenting
extremities.

***

You give only to facilitate
the process of taking.

***

Life is a long-playing
record
with a lousy needle.

***

If pain is a source
of growth
my soul
must be consuming
my flesh
with its appetite.

***

Love's vague finger points
to connections never made
and our tired boxcars
couplings linked
carry the everyday
into the commonplace.

***

He swims in my eternity.

***

Truth is not always beautiful,
but if proclaimed in love,
it transforms itself.

***

In my dark solitude
I touched a dark world
and became darkly touchable.

***

I desire only the absence
of desire
and the fullness of bleached bones.

***

This beauty pains only from
never being given away.

***

I have you in fragments.
I do not despair –
I have you everywhere.

***

Build your walls
to enclose my world.

***

Loving you shoots me skyward.

***

Truth is distilled wisdom.
Your wisdom is my truth,
my truth is your wisdom.
Together we dwell in essence.

***

Your silences darkly golden
holds my silvery moon,
a tender embrace
of the night.

***

A mother's sorrow
is a dark womb
without life.

***

To love God requires sacrifice of
the lowest elements so that we
might rise to the highest.

***

Bondage comes in many forms
and the only liberation is love.

***

To love yourself is true freedom.

***

Love – sacrifice – pain – joy –
they are all one and the same.

On the Everyday

"Make use – make use."
The world revolves repeating
"Make use, make use."

***

Laughing at ourselves
is the only means
to sanity.

***

To be alive, to breathe
in and out, can be
a travail in itself.

***

Perhaps there are limits
to being human
but I have not found them.

***

When anger enters my heart, I burn
and the fire will not
diminish unless I speak.

***

To speak anger in truth is to
free oneself from self-hate.

***

My happiness rose from my dreams today
and refused to put on a dress.

**

Stillness does not
always indicate death,
only a desiring of it.

**

A little wine,
a little soup for sustenance
is all I need
in this cold winter
of my life.

**

Courage always
seems to be
something someone
else has.

**

Even a good and
fortunate life contains
heartache few see.

**

Only as our hair
turns gray do
we realize how
much time we
have wasted.

***

Suffering can cripple.
Suffering can liberate.
The choice is ours alone.

***

The letter of the law always kills.
The spirit of the law enlivens.

***

Only a whole person can live
wholesomely.

***

Better the expanse
better the sky
better the nothingness
of holes in the dark night
bringing tomorrows
of wonder.

***

Sadness does not
need a reason,
only a purpose.

***

The snow filters
in and out of the morning
like Alencon lace
on the black velvet of my soul.

***

If I could immerse a day
I would –
dropped through heavy liquid
warmed, muted, softened
a pebble of silence,
a quiet pool,
a plenitude of peace.

***

The nothingness
is elaborate,
ain't it, love?

***

In the warm darkness
small beings
shoot forth
inexplicable life.

***

Today
never bows to my melodrama.
It comes in straight and true
without flourish
and my heart applauds.

***

Everything must be earned
it seems
except you who are,
the getting out
of all that isn't.

***

A formula: discern what I can.
Ignore what can disturb my balance
and wait for tomorrow's revelation.

***

If I must be round
make me a bird –
when I fly no one will see me
glistening in the wind
and rolling with the sky
as my bones sing.

***

I'm always braver and wiser
on paper
than I am within.
Only the Lord
hears me whimper.

***

To live without pain
or some form of suffering
seems impossible
but to live without hope
is the greatest anguish.

***

Finding my way
through the intricacies
of the moment,
I sometimes glimpse
the vast simplicity
of eternity.

***

Don't try
to "find yourself"
on this earth
when you
belong
elsewhere.

***

Build your walls
to enclose my world.

**

To be alive, to breathe
in and out, can be
a travail in itself.

**

Come now, children,
gather round Grandma's
wisdom and devour it
like you do her cookies.

**

Let me rest,
content
in the teacup
of your mind.

**

If we could be quiet,
a shush would fall
over the landscape.

Made in the USA
Middletown, DE
05 May 2018